BASEL TRAV
2024

Discover Hidden Gems And Must-See

Attractions with Essential Tips

Rita R. Nowlin

TABLE OF CONTENT

CHAPTER 1: INTRODUCTION

Overview of Basel

As I walked off the train and onto the platform of Basel's main station, I could feel the excitement rising within me. The cold Swiss air enveloped me, and the city's bustling energy drew me to explore its many attractions. My vacation to Basel was an exploration of a city that perfectly combined history, culture, and modernity.

The first thing that drew my attention was the gorgeous architecture that decorated the metropolis. Basel Cathedral stood boldly, its Gothic spires soaring towards the sky, bearing witness to centuries of history inscribed into its stones. The old town's tiny cobblestone lanes murmured tales of bygone times, beckoning me to explore its mediaeval beauty.

As I wandered along Basel's Rhine River, I was struck by the combination of modern art pieces and timeless beauty. The riverbanks were turned into outdoor galleries, demonstrating the city's dedication to embracing the avant-garde while preserving its rich cultural legacy.

The Kunstmuseum Basel, a treasure trove of art ranging from the Middle Ages to modern masterpieces, offered a visual feast that I eagerly expected. The city's dedication to the arts was evident, and I couldn't wait to immerse myself in the creative spirit that radiated from its galleries.

Basel's renown as a centre for innovation and research was reflected in its cutting-edge museums and educational facilities. The Vitra Campus, a short train trip away, provided a look into the future with its avant-garde architecture and design. The city's commitment to intellectual pursuits inspired me, and I was eager to learn more about the concepts and information that helped build Basel's identity.

As the day progressed, I found myself pulled to the bustling Marktplatz, where the Rathaus (Town Hall) stood out with its bright red front. The vibrant market square was a kaleidoscope of colours and fragrances, demonstrating the breadth of Basel's culinary culture. From classic Swiss delicacies to foreign flavours, the gourmet options promised to take my taste buds on a delicious voyage.

My time to Basel was only beginning, yet I could already see the city's distinct personality creating an unforgettable impression on me. Whether I was tracing the footprints of history in the old town or embracing the forward-thinking mentality along the Rhine, Basel had weaved its charm, and I was eager to discover more of its mysteries in the coming days.

Brief History

Basel, located on the Rhine River in Switzerland, has a 2,000-year history that includes a rich tapestry of cultural, artistic, and architectural advancements.

The city's history dates back to Roman times, when it was known as "Augusta Raurica." The well-preserved Roman theatre and archaeological ruins in adjacent Kaiseraugst provide views into a bygone period. Basel grew as a renowned mediaeval commercial town and eventually joined the strong Hanseatic League.

The University of Basel was founded in 1460, and during the Renaissance period, arts and education flourished in Basel. This intellectual hub drew renowned people such as Erasmus of Rotterdam, who left an everlasting influence on the city's cultural scene. The Basel Minster, a beautiful Gothic cathedral, exemplifies the era's architectural brilliance.

Basel became a printing industry centre in the 16th century as a result of Johannes Gutenberg's famous printing press. During the Reformation, the city was an important hub for the propagation of ideas, with leaders such as John Calvin seeking asylum here.

Fast forward to the twentieth century, and Basel's image as a cultural powerhouse was cemented with the 1970 launch of the Art Basel event. This yearly festival has since become a global hotspot for art lovers, demonstrating the city's dedication to supporting creativity and innovation.

Today, Basel flawlessly combines its historical beauty with modern elegance. The Old Town's cobblestone walkways lead to modern art institutions such as the Fondation Beyeler and the Kunstmuseum Basel. The city's devotion to sustainability and innovation is reflected in its cutting-edge architecture, which includes the Roche Tower and the Novartis Campus.

10 Reasons To Visit Basel

1. Basel has several art museums, including the prestigious Kunstmuseum and Fondation Beyeler. The city is a hotspot for art enthusiasts, with a rich collection of ancient and modern masterpieces.

2. Explore Basel's Old Town, which has well-preserved mediaeval buildings, lovely squares, and the famed Basel Minster. The architecture reflects centuries of history and lends a timeless appeal to the city.

3. The Rhine River runs through Basel, creating a picturesque background for the city. Take a leisurely stroll along the riverbanks, enjoy boat tours, or unwind at one of the numerous riverfront cafés while admiring the spectacular vistas.

4. Basel boasts a diversified culinary culture with Swiss, French, and German influences. Dine at Michelin-starred restaurants, visit local markets, and sample Swiss chocolates and pastries.

5. Basel has a diverse range of museums, including those dedicated to natural history and toys. The Swiss Architecture Museum and the Tinguely Museum, which honours the works of Jean Tinguely, are particularly significant.

6. Basel has cultural events throughout the year, including the famed Art Basel fair, which is the world's leading

contemporary art show. The city's theatres, music festivals, and events all contribute to its thriving cultural environment.

7. Basel Zoo, a family-friendly attraction, is one of the world's oldest and features a broad selection of species. It offers a thrilling experience for visitors of all ages, thanks to its well-designed ecosystems and conservation initiatives.

8. Enjoy shopping at Basel's exquisite shops and high-end businesses. The city's retail areas have a mix of worldwide brands and local handmade products, making it a haven for people looking for high-quality items.

9. Basel's strategic location makes it simple to visit surrounding sites like Germany's Black Forest, France's Alsace region, and Switzerland's Jura highlands. Short trips provide an opportunity to explore the region's variety.

10. Basel's efficient public transport infrastructure allows visitors to easily explore the city and neighbouring areas. Trams and buses effectively link significant sights, making it an easy destination for travellers.

CHAPTER 2: GETTING TO BASEL

By Air

EuroAirportBasel-Mulhouse-Freiburg(BSL): is the nearest airport to Basel, about 4 kilometres (2.5 miles) away. It is located in France, but services both Basel and Mulhouse. EuroAirport receives flights from several European locations, as well as a handful from North America and the Middle East.

Zurich Airport (ZRH): Despite being further distant (90 minutes by train), Zurich provides more flight connections, particularly to international destinations. The train ride itself is lovely, passing through the Swiss countryside.

Airport Transsfer:

From EuroAirport, take bus 50, which runs every 15 minutes and takes 20 minutes to get to Basel SBB station. Tickets cost around 7 CHF. Taxis are also available, although can be costly.

From Zurich Airport, take the train directly to Basel SBB station. Trains travel regularly, and the journey takes around 1.5 hours. Tickets may be purchased both online and at the airport station

Transportation From The Airport

By Train

Basel SBB: The city's principal railway station, Basel SBB, serves as a key hub, linking Basel to locations throughout Switzerland and Europe. Relax and enjoy the pleasant drive while taking in the changing surroundings.

By Car

Basel is situated on the borders of three countries: Switzerland, France, and Germany. This makes it easily accessible by automobile from each of the three nations. However, bear in mind that Switzerland has stringent environmental restrictions, and you may be required to pay a vignette (sticker) to drive on its highways.

Public Transportation Within Basel

Trams And Buses: Basel's tram and bus system is vast, efficient, and reasonably priced. A single ticket for one zone costs CHF 2.30, while a day ticket covering all zones costs CHF 9.90. Tickets may be purchased via machines at tram and bus stops, or via the Whim app (more on that later).

Basel is separated into zones, therefore the cost of your ticket depends on how many zones you pass through. If you're staying in the city centre, a one-zone ticket should serve for the majority of your journeys.

Mobility Pass: If you're staying at a hotel in Basel, you could be eligible for a free Mobility Pass, which provides free access to public transit during your stay. Check with your hotel for further information. Otherwise, it costs 30 CHF for 24 hours, 45 CHF for 48 hours, and 60 CHF for 72 hours.

Walking: Basel is a tiny city, so many of the important sights are within walking distance of one another. Walking is an excellent way to see the city and get some exercise.

Cycling: Basel is a bike-friendly city, with several bike rental shops where you may borrow a bike for the day. This is an excellent opportunity to discover the city at your own leisure.

E-scooters are another popular way to travel about Basel. There are various e-scooter rental firms in the city, with pricing varying based on the company and the period of the rental.

Taxis in Basel are relatively costly and should be utilised as a last option. The minimum fee is CHF 6.50, with a charge of CHF 3 per km.

CHAPTER 3:
ACCOMMODATION

Hotels in Basel

Luxury Hotels

Hotel Les Trois Rois: The hotel, with its majestic neoclassical front, is *situated in the centre of the Old Town, right on the banks of the Rhine River.* One of Basel's most historic and magnificent hotels, built in the 17th century on the riverbank. It has been visited by princes and celebrities for ages and provides a really sumptuous experience. The hotel features a Michelin-starred restaurant, a spa, and a cigar lounge. A regular double room starts at about CHF 1,000 per night. *Tel: +41 61 260 70 70*

Radisson Blu Hotel, Basel: This luxury hotel is *situated in the centre of Basel, near several of the city's prominent attractions.* It features stylish accommodations, an Italian restaurant and bar, a spa and a pool. A regular double room starts at around CHF 400 per night. *www.radissonhotels.com/en-us/hotels/radisson-blu-basel*

Hotel Märthof Basel: This old hotel is *located in the Old Town, near the Münsterplatz*. It features luxury accommodations, a gourmet restaurant, and a spa. A regular double room starts at around CHF 300 per night. *www.hotel-maerthof-basel.ch/. Tel: +41 61 261 99 33*

Hyperion Hotel Basel: This contemporary hotel is *near the Messe Basel show centre*. It features modern accommodations, a casino, a restaurant, and a bar with spectacular city views. A regular double room starts at about CHF 250 per night. *www.h-hotels.com/en/hyperion/hotels/hyperion-hotel-basel Tel: +41 61 260 12 12*

Budget-Friendly Options

ibis budget Basel City: This hotel, *located near the train station*, has modest yet clean rooms with complimentary Wi-Fi. Prices for a double room start around CHF 70 per night. *Tel: +41 61 317 4000*

easyHotel Basel: This hotel is *situated in a quiet residential area in Riehen district, about a 15-minute walk from Basel SBB train station.* It has tiny but practical rooms with complimentary Wi-Fi. Prices for a double room start around CHF 80 per night.*www.easyhotel.com/hotels/switzerland/basel/basel* *Tel: +41 61 683 55 80*

Bed And Breakfasts

HOTEL IBIS STYLES BASEL CITY: The hotel is *located near the city center, just off the A2 motorway. There is a public car park on-site, as well as street parking available.* This hotel has brightly coloured rooms, a relaxing lobby bar and free breakfast. It's an excellent alternative for individuals seeking a sophisticated and sociable environment. Price: Starting at CHF 119 per night. *www.all.accor.com/hotel/9665/index.en.shtml* *Tel: +41 61 544 0444*

B&B Hotel Basel Switzerland: *located near the airport,* offers contemporary rooms with free Wi-Fi and breakfast. Prices for a double room start around CHF 90 per night. *www.hotel-bb.com/en/hotel/basel Tel: +41 61 551 2424*

Hostels

Basel Backpacker Hostel: This hostel is *right in the middle of the city, near to all of the main attractions.* It has both dormitories and private rooms, as well as a shared kitchen, laundry facilities and a bar. Prices for a dorm bed start about CHF 35/night. *www.baselbackpack.com/ Tel: +41 61 361 71 28*

Youth Hostel Basel*: Located in a calm residential area, this hostel is yet within walking distance of the city centre.* It has both dormitories and private rooms, as well as a shared kitchen, laundry facilities, and a garden. Prices for a dorm bed start about CHF 40/night. *www.youthhostel.ch/en/hostels/basel/ Tel: +41 61 272 05 72*

St. Johann Guest House, *a historic structure in Basel's Old Town*, serves as a youth hostel. It has both dormitories and private rooms, as well as a shared kitchen, laundry facilities, and a rooftop patio. Prices for a dorm bed start about CHF 45/night. *www.pflegehotel-bs.ch/ Tel: +41 61 326 16 16*

CHAPTER 4: SIGHTSEEING AND ATTRACTIONS

Old Town (Altstadt)

Basel Minster: Begin your adventure with the renowned Basel Minster, a Got I don't know I thought makes you feel so madhic masterpiece that dominates the skyline. The elaborate embellishments on its exterior, as well as the amazing panoramic views from the towers, are nothing short of spectacular. Allow yourself time to absorb the centuries of history etched in its walls. *www.baslermuenster.ch/ Tel: +41 61 271 75 75*

Marktplatz (Market Square): Explore the busy market square with historic structures. The Rathaus (Town Hall) commands attention with its brilliant red front and finely painted paintings, which provide an insight into the city's political history. The area vibrates with the energy of both inhabitants and visitors, creating a lively environment.

Basel Historical Museum (Historisches Museum Basel): Explore the city's rich history at this museum. Housed in a mediaeval structure, the museum tells a compelling story via artefacts, paintings, and displays that transport visitors through the city's many epochs.

Basel Art Museum (Kunstmuseum Basel): With a collection ranging from the Middle Ages to modern art, this museum is a must-see for art fans. The museum's architecture is as enthralling as the artworks within, making it a cultural sanctuary in the Old Town.

Spalentor: Explore the cobblestone lanes and see Spalentor, one of the three mediaeval gates that previously secured the city. This well-preserved gate, embellished with towers and statues, serves as a reminder of Basel's mediaeval walls and an attractive photo location.

Rhine River Promenade: End your trip with a relaxing walk along the Rhine River Promenade. Admire the Old Town's silhouette from the other bank, and consider taking a boat trip or relaxing at one of the riverfront cafés, soaking in the peace that contrasts with the hustle and bustle of daily life.

Fondation Beyeler

www.fondationbeyeler.ch/. Tel: +41 61 645 97 00. The
Fondation Beyeler is well-known for its impressive collection
of modern and contemporary art, which includes works by
Claude Monet, Vincent van Gogh, Pablo Picasso, and other
notable artists. The museum's architectural brilliance,
designed by Renzo Piano, blends seamlessly with its natural
surroundings, resulting in a harmonious space that enhances
the art viewing experience.

One of the most memorable aspects of a visit to the Fondation Beyeler is the exceptional exhibition curation. The museum frequently presents temporary exhibitions that highlight a variety of creative styles, subjects, and time periods. Visitors can immerse themselves in the beauty and innovation of these carefully curated exhibits, learning about the evolution of art throughout history.

The expansive sculpture garden that surrounds the museum is another must-see. The garden is set against the backdrop of the Swiss landscape and features iconic sculptures by artists such as Alexander Calder and Ellsworth Kelly. It offers a serene setting for contemplation and reflection, as well as a one-of-a-kind fusion of art and nature.

The museum's commitment to education is reflected in its various programmes, which include guided tours, lectures, and workshops. These initiatives appeal to people of all ages, making the Fondation Beyeler a welcoming and enriching destination for families, students, and art lovers.[1]

Rheinfelden Thermal Baths

www.soleuno.ch/ Tel: +41 61 833 22 22. As you enter the thermal baths, a sensation of serenity rushes over you, accompanied by the soothing sounds of running water and the faint perfume of essential oils. The architecture flawlessly merges modern elegance and classic charm, providing a sophisticated luxury atmosphere.

When you walk into the warm, mineral-rich waters, your cares melt away and your muscles relax. Thermal waters have restorative capabilities that rejuvenate your body and invigorate your spirit. You float weightlessly, giving in to the healing embrace of the water, letting every trace of worry melt away with each soft wave.

Beyond the pools, a plethora of luxurious facilities await. From relaxing saunas to lavish spa treatments, there's something for every sense. Immerse yourself in a world of happiness as experienced therapists use their talented hands to knead away tension, leaving you feeling completely blissful.

Between luxuriant periods of relaxation, take a chance to explore the verdant surrounds. Wander through beautiful gardens, revelling in nature's splendour, or take a leisurely stroll down the riverbank, admiring the lovely scenery.

As the day comes to an end, bask in the glow of complete pleasure, knowing that you've experienced a pocket of paradise in the heart of Basel.

Basel Botanical Garden

www.botgarten.unibas.ch/ Tel: +41 61 265 56 00. One of the highlights of the Basel Botanical Garden is its wide collection of plants from all over the world. From exotic tropical species to local Swiss flora, the garden has a remarkable range of botanical variety. Wander through themed areas that take you to many parts of the world, from the Mediterranean to the Far East, highlighting the beauty and diversity of plant life on our planet.

Many people are drawn to the spectacular glasshouse, a botanical architecture marvel that allows you to immerse yourself in a tropical paradise regardless of the weather outside. Inside, you'll find towering palm trees, bright orchids, and a plethora of other tropical treasures, providing a sensory feast for the eyes and nose.

For those with an eye for the odd, the Basel Botanical Garden has a variety of rare and endangered plants, demonstrating the importance of conservation efforts in conserving our planet's biodiversity. Admire ancient cycads, delicate carnivorous plants, and rare orchid species, each having its own distinct story to tell.

As you stroll down meandering walkways and quiet ponds, take advantage of one of the garden's lovely picnic areas or tranquil seats to rest and decompress. Whether you want to relax in nature or go on a botanical excursion with family and friends, the Basel Botanical Garden has something for everyone.

Basel Zoo

www.zoobasel.ch/ Tel:+41 61 295 35 35

1. **Diverse Habitats:** Basel Zoo boasts a varied range of environments. From the lush foliage of the Monkey House to the simulated underwater settings of the Aquarium, each segment takes visitors to different parts of the world, highlighting our planet's remarkable biodiversity.

2. **Etosha**: The Etosha exhibit is a detailed replica of the African savannah, making it a centrepiece of the zoo. Here, stately giraffes, beautiful zebras, and intimidating elephants walk freely in an environment that mimics their natural

habitat. The immersive experience allows you to see these wonderful species up close while also appreciating the grandeur of Africa's ecology.

3. **Penguin World** offers a flavour of the Southern Hemisphere. Watch with joy as lively penguins frolic in an environment built to resemble Antarctica's frigid surroundings. Educational displays give insights into the life of these attractive birds, making it a worthwhile experience for both children and adults.

4. **Masoala Rainforest**: Explore an indoor tropical paradise replicating Madagascar's rich greenery and vivid fauna. Wander through the foggy passageways, surrounded by exotic flora, and meet lemurs, chameleons, and other intriguing species in a setting that mimics their natural habitat.

5. **Vivarium:** The Basel Zoo's Vivarium features a diverse collection of reptiles, amphibians, and invertebrates. This region is ideal for people with a strong interest in lesser-known but equally intriguing inhabitants of the animal world. From writhing snakes to brightly coloured frogs, the

Vivarium provides a unique view on the world of cold-blooded species.

6. **Zolli Playground**: For families with children, the Zolli Playground offers a pleasant and safe space to burn off energy. This play area, located inside the zoo grounds, has animal-themed buildings and games that give an added layer of fun to your visit.

7. **Flamingo Lagoon**: Experience the beauty of the Flamingo Lagoon, home to exquisite pink flamingos. The lagoon's placid environment allows for peaceful observation, making it an ideal place to enjoy the elegance and beauty of these bird occupants.

8. **Interactive displays**: The Basel Zoo offers several interactive displays and educational programmes that promote wildlife conservation. From guided tours to informational signs, the zoo invites visitors to have a better appreciation of the value of maintaining our planet's biodiversity.

St Paul Church

www.kulturkirche-paulus.ch/ Tel: +41 61 272 88 88. As you approach, take a minute to admire the delicate features of its exterior and the majestic tower that soars for the sky.

When you enter the church, you will be enveloped in a peaceful and spiritually significant environment. The inside features beautiful stained glass windows that fill the area with a kaleidoscope of colours, producing a mesmerising dance of light. These windows not only tell biblical stories, but also serve as marvels of creative expression, demonstrating the ability of craftsmen throughout history.

One of the main attractions in St. Paul's Church is the remarkable organ, which is known for its superb craftsmanship and strong reverberation. Whether you enjoy music or not, the majesty of the organ will definitely inspire you. If you have the opportunity, witnessing a musical performance in a church may be a genuinely amazing experience, since the acoustics enhance the beauty of the tunes.

The church's historical significance is heightened by its function as the final resting place for prominent personalities from Basel's history. As you go through the aisles, you'll notice memorial plaques and graves dedicated to notable figures, which give a layer of cultural complexity to your visit.

St. Paul's Church is more than just a historical site; it is still engaged in the community. Check the calendar for religious services, concerts, and events, as these occasions offer a rare opportunity to see the church come to life with the energy of modern activities.

Toy World Museum

www.spielzeug-welten-museum-basel.ch/ Tel: +41 (0)61 225 95 95. As you enter the museum, you are met by an immersive environment that transports you back in time. One of the main attractions is the Vintage Toy Collection, which features painstakingly maintained toys from previous eras. From traditional wooden dolls and tin soldiers to highly built model railroads, each display offers a tale about past playtimes.

The interactive Play Zone is the museum's standout feature, allowing visitors to participate in hands-on activities and rediscover the excitement of traditional games. This portion not only appeals to children, but also allows adults to revisit their favourite childhood experiences, creating a sense of shared nostalgia.

For anyone interested in the evolution of toys over time, the Toy History Wing is a must-see. Here, you may follow the evolution of notable toys and see how societal changes affected playthings. The exhibits offer an intriguing view into the cultural significance of toys, emphasising their function as more than just enjoyment.

The Basel Toy World Museum also has a cutting-edge Virtual Reality (VR) experience that allows visitors to put themselves in the shoes of toy designers and watch the creative process that goes into making cherished toys. It's an inventive addition that combines the allure of heritage with the wonders of modern technology.

A tour around the museum's Artistic Creations Gallery reveals the skills of professional toymakers, who demonstrate meticulous workmanship and inventive ideas. This section demonstrates the creative value contained in each toy, transforming them into little pieces of art.

To make your visit even more memorable, try participating in one of the museum's seminars or activities. These engaging courses provide a more in-depth understanding of the world of toys, promoting active engagement and developing a feeling of community among attendees.

Antikenmuseum Basel

www.antikenmuseumbasel.ch/ Tel: +41 61 266 56 66. Upon entering the museum, tourists are instantly captivated to the magnificent collection of artefacts from many cultures and ages. One of the main attractions is the Greek and Roman Antiquities display, which features wonderfully preserved sculptures, ceramics, and everyday things that provide insight into the daily lives and artistic triumphs of these ancient civilizations.

Another highlight is the museum's Egyptian Collection, which features a fascinating collection of mummies, sculptures, and artefacts that transport visitors back in time to the pharaohs and pyramids. The rich intricacies and symbolic importance of each piece make this show a must-see for anybody interested in ancient Egyptian secrets.

The Antikenmuseum Basel also has an impressive collection of Near Eastern artefacts, including Mesopotamian and Persian artefacts. Visitors may marvel at the ancient cuneiform tablets, towering reliefs, and elaborate jewellery that narrate the stories of these ancient civilizations, giving them a thorough grasp of their cultural achievements.

Furthermore, the museum often holds special exhibitions and activities, which allow visitors to dive further into various parts of antiquity. These temporary exhibits enrich the overall experience by presenting a dynamic and evolving display of the museum's enormous collection.

Dreiländereck

www.basBorder-trel.com/wen/Media/Attractions/Leisure-time-excursions/iangle. This geographical juncture, commonly known as the "Three-Country Corner," is situated at the confluence of the Rhine and Wiese rivers. Here is an evocative investigation of the Dreiländereck in Basel.

At Dreiländereck, you may experience the convergence of three unique cultures and nationalities. The symbolic confluence of Switzerland, Germany, and France produces a one-of-a-kind ambiance that displays Europe's rich variety.

The Dreiländereck, located along the Rhine River, offers stunning panoramic views. Take a leisurely stroll down the riverbanks and soak in the tranquil beauty of the flowing waterways, surrounded by magnificent scenery that flawlessly merge the natural components of three different countries.

The Dreiländereck is distinguished by a unique monument with the flags of Switzerland, Germany, and France. This landmark symbolises the solidarity and closeness of two neighbouring nations. Capture the occasion with images at this landmark location that depicts the meeting place of boundaries.

Explore the cultural differences of each nation represented at the Dreiländereck. Engage with the people and admire the diverse mix of languages, cultures, and traditions that live at this peaceful intersection. This is a fantastic opportunity to explore Basel's distinct charm, a city that thrives on its cosmopolitan culture.

Recreational activities include picnics at adjacent parks and boat cruises along the Rhine. Consider taking a boat excursion to see the picturesque splendour of the river that unites these three nations.

Explore the historical importance of Dreiländereck, including how political boundaries have changed throughout time. Learn about the common history of Switzerland, Germany, and France, and appreciate the harmonious coexistence that defines this area.

The Dreiländereck offers a delicious combination of Swiss, German, and French cuisines. Local restaurants and cafés in the area offer the opportunity to sample the various flavours that distinguish each country's culinary history.

Neighborhood Of St. Alban

St. Alban Gate (St. Alban-Tor): Begin your trip with the landmark St. Alban Gate, a well-preserved mediaeval gate that serves as the entrance to the St. Alban neighbourhood. The gate's mediaeval construction reflects Basel's historical significance and provides a lovely starting place for your journey.

St. Alban Church (St. Alban Kirche): St. Alban Church, located in the centre of the neighbourhood, is a Gothic architectural marvel. The church, which dates back to the 11th century, has stunning stained glass windows, ornate sculptures, and a peaceful atmosphere. Take a moment to absorb the spiritual and historical atmosphere of this cultural treasure.

St. Alban Teich (St. Alban Pond): St. Alban Teich is a picturesque pond surrounded by greenery that offers a peaceful escape. It's the perfect place for a relaxing stroll, a calm picnic, or simply admiring the natural splendour. The contrast of this tranquil oasis against the backdrop of the city adds to the neighborhood's allure.

Museum Tinguely: Art enthusiasts will enjoy Museum Tinguely, which is dedicated to the works of Swiss artist Jean Tinguely. The museum houses an intriguing collection of kinetic art, sculptures, and drawings, offering a unique perspective on the intersection of art and technology. *www.tinguely.ch/en Tel: +41 61 681 93 20 and +41 61 688 94 49.*

Rhine River Promenade: St. Alban is perfectly located along the Rhine River, providing a breathtaking riverside promenade. Take a leisurely walk along the riverbanks, enjoy the view of the Rhine, and perhaps dine on the waterfront. The promenade offers a refreshing respite and an opportunity to appreciate Basel's natural beauty.

St. Alban Rheinweg: This quaint street is lined with historic buildings, boutiques, and cafes. Wander through St Alban Rheinweg to soak up the local atmosphere, discover unique shops and enjoy a cup of coffee at a pavement café. The street's cobblestone charm contributes to the neighborhood's overall allure.

Culinary Delights: St. Alban has a diverse culinary scene. Explore the local restaurants and eateries to sample Swiss specialties or international cuisine. The neighborhood's gastronomic offerings enrich your visit by allowing you to sample Basel's diverse culinary traditions.

Basel Paper Mill

www.baslerpapiermuehle.ch/ Tel: +41 61 261 56 56. The Basel Paper Mill, established in the 15th century, is one of Switzerland's oldest paper mills. As you enter this ancient building, you'll be immersed in the progression of paper-making skills and the cultural significance they possessed at various times.

Take a guided tour to completely understand the intricate process of paper making. Knowledgeable experts will tour you through the whole process, from raw materials to finished product, revealing the workmanship and innovations that have moulded the paper industry over centuries.

The mill offers interactive displays to interest visitors of all ages. You may see demonstrations of classic paper-making processes, gaining hands-on experience with the creativity involved in producing this crucial material.

The Basel Paper Mill hosts modern paper work and exhibitions, in addition to its historical significance. The venue frequently holds exhibitions demonstrating the flexibility of paper as a medium of artistic expression. These displays help to shape Basel's dynamic and growing cultural scene.

The on-site paper shop provides a unique way to acquire handmade paper items. From finely produced stationery to art prints, you may take home a piece of the mill's history. It's the ideal location to find unique souvenirs or presents that showcase the beauty of traditional papermaking.

The Basel Paper Mill, located along the Rhine River, offers a magnificent setting for visitors. The combination of ancient buildings and natural beauty adds to the overall aura, offering a peaceful setting for exploration and reflection.

The mill provides educational programmes and seminars for schools and hobbyists alike. These programmes provide a greater knowledge of the cultural and technological components of paper manufacture, making it an ideal location for both pleasure and education.

Explore the paper mill's history and inventiveness, then unwind at the on-site café. Enjoy a cup of coffee while taking in the peaceful surroundings, making your visit a complete and delightful experience.

Tinguely Fountain

www.basel.com/en/attractions/tinguely-fountain. The elaborate and continually moving mechanical sculptures that surround the Tinguely Fountain are one of its most outstanding characteristics. The fountain is ornamented with a collection of colourful and amusing metal figurines that are propelled by the power of water. These dynamic sculptures come to life, forming a captivating dance of metal, water, and light. Each item is precisely crafted to move in sync with the flow of water, creating a visually spectacular and engaging experience.

As you explore the Tinguely Fountain, you will be captivated by the sculptures' rhythmic and surprising motions. The interaction between the mechanical parts and the surrounding water evokes surprise and interest. It's more than simply a fountain; it's a living, breathing work of art that stimulates all of your senses.

The Tinguely Fountain is especially notable since it is located on the Rhine River near the Tinguely Museum. This adds another depth to your experience by allowing you to simply explore the museum itself. The museum is dedicated to the life and works of Jean Tinguely, and it offers significant insights into the artist's creative process and progress.

Furthermore, the Tinguely Fountain acts as a focal point for social interaction and leisure. Visitors frequently congregate around the fountain to admire its beauty, snap pictures, or simply relax in the peaceful surroundings. The sound of water splashing and mechanical motions create a relaxing atmosphere, making it a great place to take a break and observe the merging of art and nature.

s

Merian Garden

www.meriangaerten.ch/. Tel: +41 61 261 04 54. When you enter the Merian Garden, the first thing you notice is the perfectly maintained grounds. The garden's design represents a perfect combination of art and nature, offering a peaceful respite from the city. Stroll down the twisting trails and you'll see a variety of brilliant blooms, aromatic herbs, and towering trees, creating a stunning environment that varies with the seasons.

One of the Merian Garden's main attractions is the Palm House, a stunning glass building that contains a wide assortment of exotic plants. Step inside and be transported to diverse climates, marvelling at the tropical vegetation that thrives in this regulated habitat. The Palm House's architectural elegance enhances the garden's overall attractiveness.

Another attraction is the Merian Grotto, which is a manmade cave with beautiful rock formations and flowing water elements. This fanciful artwork honours the 17th-century practice of making grottoes as emblems of mystery and beauty in gardens. It offers a unique and evocative environment for tourists to explore.

For people interested in cultural history, the Merian Garden includes the Merian Park, which displays the remnants of the once-mighty Augusta Raurica. This archaeological site offers a look into Basel's Roman history, with well-preserved remains and artefacts illustrating the narrative of the old community.

As you go around the garden, you'll notice fascinating sculptures and secret corners that contribute to the overall appeal. The Merian Garden is more than simply a botanical marvel; it's also a living canvas that honours the relationship between nature and art.

Tier Park Lange Erlen

www.erlen-verein.ch/ Tel: +41 61 692 75 35. Tierpark Lange Erlen offers scenic beauty, including rich foliage, stunning vistas, and tranquil walking pathways. The park's design invites people to take leisurely strolls and absorb themselves in the beauty of their surroundings.

The park's diversified animal population attracts wildlife enthusiasts. Tierpark Lange Erlen allows visitors to watch and learn about a variety of animals in their natural habitat, including local species and exotic critters. Deer, wild boars, and several bird species are common occupants.

Families with children will love the well-maintained playgrounds located throughout the park. Tierpark Lange Erlen is a family-friendly location since these areas are specifically created to engage children.

Picnic areas provide a natural setting for tourists to relax and enjoy their meals. Bring some snacks or a picnic basket and take use of the well-kept picnic sites for a relaxing outdoor meal.

Tierpark Lange Erlen offers educational programmes in addition to its recreational activities. The park provides a variety of programmes and activities, many of which are created specifically for schools and educational groups, to raise awareness about animal conservation and environmental issues.

The park's calm atmosphere is enhanced by its attractive pond and water features. The water features attract a variety of bird species, adding to the park's overall biological richness.

The park is designed to accommodate individuals of all ages and abilities. Tierpark Lange Erlen's natural beauty is easily accessible thanks to well-maintained walkways, benches, and amenities.

The park may feature festivals, nature walks, or educational seminars based on the season. Check the park's schedule to see if there are any special events happening during your visit.

Rhine River Cruises

As you float over the peaceful Rhine, Basel's outstanding sights, such as the magnificent Basel Minster and the renowned Rathaus, wish you farewell. Soon, you'll be immersed in a storybook setting, with luscious vineyards covering the slopes and charming towns dotting the riverbanks.

The picturesque village of Breisach awaits, with its centuries-old church soaring above the cobblestone lanes. Visit a local vineyard to learn about the region's rich winemaking history and sip beautiful wines while admiring panoramic views of the vine-clad slopes.

Continuing upstream, the famed Black Forest beckons with its lush forests and fairytale towns. Don't pass up the opportunity to savour a slice of classic Black Forest cake with a hot cup of coffee, a rich delicacy that wonderfully captures the region's gastronomic delights.

As the cruise heads near Strasbourg, France, you'll be captivated by the city's fairytale-like appeal, complete with half-timbered homes and meandering canals. Explore the UNESCO-listed Grande Île, where centuries of history are brought to life by architectural wonders such as the breathtaking Strasbourg Cathedral.

Further along the path, the beautiful city of Cologne, Germany, awaits, with its distinctive twin-spired cathedral dominating the landscape. Explore the city's colourful culture by taking a stroll along the bustling waterfront promenade or sampling local foods at one of the boisterous beer gardens.

As your voyage comes to an end, Amsterdam appears on the horizon, with its distinctive canal belt and ancient sites providing a perfect conclusion to your Rhine River experience. Whether you're admiring world-class art at the Van Gogh Museum or simply taking in the laid-back atmosphere of this delightful city, Amsterdam promises to be an outstanding end to your cruise.

Outdoor activities

Scavenger Hunt

A Basel Scavenger Hunt allows you to unleash your inner explorer!

Imagine winding around Basel's lovely streets while actively partaking in an exciting puzzle adventure. That is the beauty of a scavenger hunt! Here's why you should think about this fun outdoor sport.

Forget the conventional tourist path. Scavenger hunts take you to lesser-known nooks, odd statuary, and historical elements that you would otherwise miss. You'll experience

Basel through new eyes, uncovering hidden treasures in plain sight.

Be a playful detective:
Crack codes, solve puzzles, and follow cryptic instructions. Each task becomes a mini-quest that piques your interest and transforms the city into a big puzzle board. It's like being in your own personal escape room, with all of Basel as your playground!

Embrace friendly competition.
Gather your friends or family and turn Basel into your own gaming arena. Collaborate, strategize, and laugh along the way. The fun rivalry heightens the excitement, resulting in memories that will live long after the hunt is ended.

Tailored experiences for everyone.
Choose between several themes and difficulty levels. Whether you're a history buff, an art enthusiast, or just looking for some family fun, a scavenger hunt is ready to pique your interest. Some even use augmented reality to lend a futuristic spin to the traditional adventure.

Benefits beyond hunting:

You'll discover intriguing things about Basel's history, culture, and landmarks in an entertaining and engaging manner. Furthermore, the physical activity allows you to enjoy the fresh air and get some exercise while seeing the city.

Rafting Tour On River Rhine

Picture yourself in the middle of breathtaking natural beauty, with the flowing waters of the Rhine serving as the perfect background for an amazing outdoor adventure.

As you begin your rafting excursion, excitement will rush through your veins as you manage the river's whirling currents and rapids. Expert guides will lead the trip, assuring your safety and fun while paddling across the gorgeous waterways.

Rafting on the Rhine provides a unique viewpoint of Basel's surrounds, allowing you to appreciate the beauty of the region from a completely different angle. Glide by stunning vistas, rich vegetation, and quaint villages that line the riverbanks, generating a sense of calm despite the excitement of the experience.

Whether you're a seasoned rafter searching for an adrenaline rush or a beginner hoping for an amazing experience, a rafting excursion on the Rhine will leave you with memories to last a lifetime. So, grab your paddle and prepare to embark on an amazing voyage down one of Europe's most renowned rivers while immersing yourself in the natural delights of Basel and the surrounding area.

Weidling Tour

Weidling, which refers to a traditional wooden boat, provides a peaceful and picturesque journey along the Rhine River, with breathtaking views of Basel's skyline and surroundings.

As you embark on this adventure, you'll be greeted by the gentle swaying of the boat and the soothing sounds of the water, creating a tranquil atmosphere that transports you away from the hustle and bustle of city life. The knowledgeable guides will entertain you with fascinating stories and anecdotes about Basel's rich history, while pointing out notable landmarks and hidden gems along the riverbanks.

One of the highlights of the Weidling tour is the chance to see Basel's iconic bridges from a different perspective. Glide effortlessly beneath majestic structures like the Middle Bridge and the Johanniterbrücke, admiring their architectural grandeur as they gracefully span the river below.

Throughout the journey, you will come across charming waterfront neighbourhoods, verdant parks, and historic buildings, all of which add to Basel's charm and character. Keep an eye out for local wildlife, such as graceful swans and playful river otters, which will add to the natural beauty of your surroundings.

As the tour comes to an end, you'll be reluctantly saying goodbye to the tranquil waters of the Rhine, but with a newfound appreciation for Basel's allure and allure.

CHAPTER 5: CULTURAL EXPERIENCES

Art Basel

Art Basel is more than just an art fair; it's a cultural extravaganza that transports you to the vibrant world of contemporary art like no other event. Visiting Basel during Art Basel is like entering a kaleidoscope of creativity, with new artistic wonders around every corner waiting to be discovered.

As you walk through Basel's bustling streets during this time, you can feel the city pulsating with energy and excitement. Galleries, museums, and exhibition spaces are brimming with masterpieces from established and emerging artists, representing a wide range of mediums and styles.

The atmosphere is electric, with the hum of conversations in multiple languages as art lovers from all over the world gather to celebrate creativity in all its forms. It's more than just looking at art; it's about engaging with it, discussing its meaning and significance, and connecting with other fans who share your enthusiasm.

Art Basel transforms Basel into a cultural melting pot, erasing traditional boundaries and fostering innovation. Whether you're admiring a provocative installation, pondering a thought-provoking sculpture, or getting lost in a captivating painting, each encounter leaves an indelible impression on your artistic sensibilities.

Beyond the exhibitions, Art Basel hosts a plethora of events, ranging from panel discussions and artist talks to performances and parties, resulting in a dynamic tapestry of experiences catering to every artistic inclination.

Perhaps the most magical aspect of Art Basel is how it transcends the art world and pervades every aspect of Basel's cultural landscape. From the architecture of its historic buildings to the flavours of its cuisine, the city transforms into a living canvas, infused with the spirit of creativity and imagination.

Theater Basel

Theatre Basel is more than just a performance; it is an immersive cultural experience that reflects Basel's rich history and contemporary spirit. When you walk into the theatre, you're greeted by an atmosphere charged with anticipation and creativity.

The theatre itself is a masterpiece, combining modern architecture with traditional elements to reflect Basel's eclectic character. Its sleek design and cutting-edge amenities promise an evening of visual and auditory delight.

But it's not just the physical space; it's the performances that bring it to life. Theatre Basel is well-known for its diverse repertoire, which ranges from classical masterpieces to avant-garde productions. Whether it's Shakespearean dramas, experimental dance performances, or cutting-edge contemporary plays, each show takes you on a journey through the depths of human emotion and thought.

What truly distinguishes Theatre Basel is its commitment to innovation and collaboration. Here, world-class artists are pushing the boundaries of their craft, creating unforgettable moments that challenge, provoke, and inspire. The combination of various art forms, languages, and cultures adds layers of complexity and richness to all performances.

Furthermore, seeing a show at Theatre Basel is a shared experience. You're more than just a spectator; you're a part of a dynamic audience that feels the performance's excitement and energy. Whether you're participating in post-show discussions, mingling in the foyer, or simply enjoying the atmosphere, you're bound to meet other culture enthusiasts from all walks of life.

And don't forget about Basel itself, a city steeped in history while pulsating with modernity. After the show, you can explore its charming streets, indulge in gourmet delights, or simply soak in the picturesque views of the Rhine. The theater becomes a gateway to the cultural tapestry of Basel, inviting you to delve deeper into its treasures.

Music And Festivals

BScene is a two-day event held in April that immerses you in the heart of Basel's local music scene. Discover emerging artists and renowned bands from a variety of genres, including rock, pop, electronic, and hip-hop. Imagine enthusiastic crowds moving to the beat, the air filled with anticipation, and the city's clubs converted into vivid stages.

FLOSS Festival: Enjoy the summer weather at FLOSS, a free open-air event staged on a floating stage on the Rhine River in August. Local and international artists enchant you with their music, resulting in a relaxed Mediterranean environment. Imagine yourself sitting on the riverfront steps, with the lovely breeze carrying the music and the cityscape glimmering in the backdrop.

Baloise session, held every October, transforms Basel into a music lover's paradise. Intimate performances with renowned performers from across the world take place in various settings throughout the city, providing an unrivalled opportunity to engage with the music and the musicians. Consider the quiet expectation in a candlelight hall, the artist's voice filling the air, and the collective feeling of musical magic.

Basel Tattoo

This yearly event features the greatest in military music, precise marching, and lively performances from all around the world.

As you enter the stadium, you're met by the thunderous pounding of drums, the melancholy strains of bagpipes, and the majestic sight of performers dressed in colourful costumes. The atmosphere is electric as you watch marching bands from many countries perform with precision and discipline, each bringing its own flare and character to the stage.

The Basel Tattoo is more than simply music and marching; it's a celebration of cultural interchange and solidarity. You'll be taken away by the artists' enthusiasm and passion as they share their culture via song, dance, and storytelling. Whether it's the passionate songs of a Scottish pipe band, the exquisite choreography of a Swiss traditional dance team, or the explosive acrobatics of a visiting international act, each moment demonstrates the power of cultural expression.

Beyond the performances, the Basel Tattoo provides an opportunity to meet with individuals from all walks of life, forming friendships that cross language and boundaries. Whether you're conversing with other audience members at interval or having a meal with the actors after the play, you'll be surrounded by a warm and welcoming Swiss atmosphere.

Basel Fasnacht (Carnival)

Fasnacht is a colourful festival held annually in Basel, Switzerland, beginning on the Monday after Ash Wednesday and lasting precisely 72 hours.

The mood during Basel Fasnacht is nothing short of electric. When you go into the streets of Basel at this period, you are instantly immersed in a maelstrom of colour, sound, and excitement. Drums beat rhythmically, piccolos play bright tunes, and revellers yell joyfully.

One of the most distinguishing elements of Basel Fasnacht is the elaborate and detailed costumes worn by the participants, known as Fasnächtlers. These costumes sometimes include intricate masks, which are beautifully constructed pieces of art in themselves. Each mask conveys a tale, whether it depicts a classic character from Basel folklore or a modern figure reflecting current events.

As you go through the streets, you'll see colourful processions called as "Cortèges" with groups of Fasnächtler marching in order and beautiful floats decked with exquisite decorations. The artistry and workmanship on exhibit are simply beautiful, and each detail is rich with significance and meaning.

However, Basel Fasnacht is more than simply a show; it is also a time of solidarity and togetherness. Locals open their houses to both friends and visitors, asking them to participate in the celebrations and sample traditional meals and drinks. The attitude of inclusion and warmth is evident, and it's easy to feel at home amidst the festivities.

The "Morgenstreich," the ceremonial inauguration of Basel Fasnacht, takes place early Monday morning. As the clock strikes 4:00 a.m., the entire city goes dark, with the only light coming from the lanterns carried by the Fasnächtler as they march through the streets. It's a strange and amazing sensation, as if you've been transported to another universe entirely.

CHAPTER 6: SHOPPING IN BASEL

Freie Strasse

As you go down Freie Strasse, you'll come across a wealth of businesses, ranging from high-end designer labels to lovely small boutiques selling unique homemade things. The stores entice you in with their alluring displays, which showcase the newest trends in fashion, accessories, jewellery, and more.

The atmosphere is vibrant, with discussion and laughter filling the air as both residents and visitors enjoy the pleasures of retail therapy. There's a sense of adventure around every turn, as you discover hidden jewels and one-of-a-kind treasures that you won't find anywhere.

Let us not forget about the gastronomic pleasures! Alongside the stores, you'll discover small cafés and diners serving wonderful snacks to fuel your shopping expedition. Whether it's a delicious chunk of Swiss chocolate or a freshly made cup of coffee, there's something to fulfil every appetite.

But arguably the most enticing part of shopping on Freie Strasse is the sense of history that pervades the entire block. As you meander through its historic streets, you can't help but feel linked to Basel's rich legacy, with each building telling stories from centuries before.

Marktplatz

Marktplatz, or Market Square, is the core of Basel's retail district, with a wide variety of stores, kiosks, and vendors selling anything from fresh vegetables and local delicacies to distinctive handcrafted crafts and souvenirs. The area itself is frequently buzzing with activity, with both residents and tourists examining the wares on display and taking in the lively atmosphere.

One of the attractions of shopping at Marktplatz is the ability to try and purchase traditional Swiss items like as cheeses, chocolates, and timepieces, all of which are well-known for their quality and workmanship. Whether you're searching for a gourmet treat to take home or a one-of-a-kind present for a loved one, there are plenty of alternatives to pique your interest and meet your shopping needs.

In addition to the market booths, Marktplatz is bordered by a wide range of stores and boutiques, from high-end luxury brands to small artisan enterprises. Whether you're looking for designer clothing, handcrafted jewellery, or one-of-a-kind home decor, you'll find something to fit your style and budget.

In addition to shopping, visiting Marktplatz allows you to immerse yourself in Basel's local culture and environment. Take a minute to appreciate the ancient architecture of the surrounding buildings, visit adjacent sites like as the Basel Town Hall and the Cathedral, and perhaps even have a leisurely meal or coffee at one of the delightful cafés or restaurants strewn about the area.

St. Johanns-Park Shopping District

A multitude of boutiques, specialised stores and wonderful eateries await your exploration.

Imagine wandering by magnificent boutiques decked with the most recent fashion trends, showing Swiss workmanship at its finest. From luxury brand labels to one-of-a-kind local treasures, there's something for everyone's style and taste. Whether you're looking for trendy clothing, gorgeous jewellery, or handcrafted items, you'll be spoilt for choice in this thriving retail district.

However, the attractiveness of St. Johanns-Park extends beyond retail therapy. As you walk around the neighbourhood, you'll come across beautiful squares and verdant parks, which provide for the ideal setting for a leisurely day of exploring. Take a minute to enjoy the ancient architecture that lines the streets, with each building conveying a unique tale about Basel's rich cultural past.

Let's not overlook the gastronomic delights that greet you around every bend. Treat yourself to a luscious Swiss chocolate delight, or savour the flavours of local food at one of the quaint cafés or restaurants scattered across the neighbourhood. Whether you're looking for a small snack or a luxury dining experience, St. Johanns-Park has lots to offer.

As the sun sets, the atmosphere of the area changes, with glittering lights providing a lovely glow over the cobblestone streets. Take your time to take up the magical environment, perhaps stopping for a glass of wine at a cosy wine bar or enjoying a leisurely evening stroll beneath the stars.

CHAPTER 7: DINING AND CUISINE

Swiss Cuisine

Local Basel Specialties

Basler Läckerli: These are classic Swiss biscuits originating in Basel. They are created with honey, almonds, candied peel, and Kirsch (cherry brandy), giving them a sweet and spicy flavour. Basler Läckerli are popular during Christmastime, although they are also available year-round at Basel's bakeries.

Basler Leckerli: Like Basler Läckerli, they are thin, crispy biscuits prepared with honey, almonds, and spices. They are frequently served with coffee or tea as a snack.

Basler Mehlsuppe: This classic Swiss soup has flour, onions, butter, and beef or vegetable stock. It's thickened with flour and spiced with nutmeg, giving it a substantial and comforting taste. Basler Mehlsuppe is frequently served as an appetiser at holiday gatherings or as a warming meal in the winter months.

Basler Rösti: While Rösti is a popular Swiss dish throughout the country, Basel offers a unique variant worth tasting. Basler Rösti is produced by frying grated potatoes till crispy and golden brown. It's frequently served as a side dish or topped with cheese, bacon, or fried eggs for a filling supper.

Baslerstab: This classic Swiss sausage is popular in Basel. It is prepared with pig and beef, spiced with nutmeg and coriander, and filled into natural casings. Baslerstab sausages are usually grilled or fried and served with mustard and toast.

Basler Fasnachtschüechli: These are deep-fried pastries eaten during Fasnacht, Basel's colourful funfair festival. Fasnachtschüechli are created by shaping a dough of flour, water, and yeast into rectangles and deep-frying them till golden brown. They are sprinkled with powdered sugar and frequently served warm as a sweet treat during carnival celebrations.

Basler Braunsauce: This classic Swiss brown sauce is popular in Basel. It is cooked with a rich beef or veal stock that is flavoured with onions, carrots, and herbs and thickened with flour or cornflour. Basler Braunsauce is frequently served alongside meat dishes like as sausages or veal schnitzel, providing depth and richness to the meal.

Restaurants and Cafés

Fine Dining

Oliv: This trendy restaurant serves Mediterranean-inspired cuisine with an emphasis on fresh fish.

Le Colombier: This delightful restaurant offers classic French cuisine in a cosy and quiet atmosphere.

Restaurant Atelier: This inventive restaurant serves a seasonal tasting menu.

Budget-Friendly Eateries

McDonald's: You can purchase a combination meal for about 15 CHF.

Pizza Hut: A big pizza costs around 15-21 CHF.

Döner Kebabs: These are available around the city and cost roughly 8-10 CHF.

Brotli Bar offers open-faced sandwiches for 3.50 CHF each.

Ganapathy serves Indian cuisine for 11 CHF each dish.

Markthalle: This indoor market features several food vendors serving a range of cuisines. You may find something for between 10 and 15 CHF.

Lunch specials: Many restaurants have fixed-price menus around lunchtime, which is an excellent way to save money. These normally cost between 20 and 30 CHF.

Nightlife in Basel

Bars and Pubs

Bar Rouge: This rooftop bar provides amazing views of the city and the Rhine River. They provide a variety of drinks, wines, and beers, as well as a menu of light nibbles.

Valentino's Place: This American-style pub is a favourite hangout for sports fans and live music enthusiasts. They provide a diverse assortment of beers, drinks, and wines, as well as burgers, pizzas, and other American staples.

Flanagan's: This cosy, wood-lined Irish bar is popular with both locals and visitors. They provide a diverse range of beers, whiskies, and other Irish beverages, as well as traditional pub cuisine such as fish & chips and shepherd's pie.

Mr. Pickwick, Pub Basel: This British pub is an excellent choice for anyone seeking a typical pub experience. They provide a diverse assortment of beers on tap, as well as pub favourites such as burgers, bangers & mash, and fish and chips.

The Pub: This British bar in the heart of Basel's Old Town is a favourite place to people watch. They provide a diverse assortment of beers on tap, as well as pub favourites such as burgers, fish & chips, and pies.

Zum **Bierjohann**: This classic Swiss brewery and bar is an excellent spot to sample local brews. They feature a large assortment of their own beers on tap, as well as a cuisine featuring Swiss favourites like sausages, cheese fondue, and rösti.

Clubs and Late-Night Venues

Nordstern: This popular floating nightclub on the Rhine River is a must-see for techno and house music enthusiasts. Dance beneath the stars on the outside terrace or immerse yourself in the throbbing beats inside.

Elysia: Immerse yourself in the mesmerising world of techno at Elysia, located in the vibrant Dreispitz neighbourhood.

Renowned DJs and cutting-edge sound equipment provide a memorable experience.

Stahlwerk: This industrial-chic club is ideal for techno purists. Prepare for strong rhythms, mesmerising light effects, and a lively audience that will dance till morning.

Heimat: This versatile venue presents a wide spectrum of live music performances, from indie bands to jazz ensembles, resulting in an intimate and thrilling ambiance.

Birds Eye Jazz Club: Immerse yourself in the soulful sounds of live jazz at Bird's Eye, a former prison gym that has been converted into a pleasant pub with a relaxing atmosphere.

CHAPTER 8: DAY TRIPS
FROM BASEL

Rhine Falls

Taking a day trip to Rhine Falls from Basel is like entering a world of breathtaking beauty. As you leave the city and head towards this natural treasure, the anticipation grows with each passing mile. The environment gradually alters, revealing stunning scenes of lush flora and flowing rivers.

When you first arrive to Rhine Falls, the sight of the falling waters takes your breath away. The sheer strength and grandeur of Europe's greatest waterfall are really breathtaking. Standing on the observation platforms, you can feel the mist on your face and hear the thunderous roar of the falls reverberating throughout the canyon.

The experience is about immersing oneself in nature's magnificence rather than simply viewing it from a distance. You may take an exhilarating boat ride up close to the thunderous waterfall, feeling the spray on your skin and marvelling at the sheer intensity of the flowing water.

Hiking routes lure those looking for a fresh viewpoint, taking them through beautiful forests and providing panoramic views of the falls from above. Each step reveals fresh beauties, from secret overlooks to peaceful picnic areas where you may enjoy the tranquilly of the surrounds.

As you tour Rhine Falls, you can't help but feel a strong connection to the natural environment. It's a place where time appears to stand still, problems fall away, and the beauty of the moment envelopes you entirely.

Black Forest (Germany)

As you leave Basel, the cool morning air fills you with excitement, and the scenery quickly turns into a gorgeous spectacle of rolling hills and green forests. When you arrive in the heart of the Black Forest, you are met with towering pine trees, their branches swinging softly in the breeze like dancers in a forest symphony.

Begin your trip by visiting one of the region's lovely towns, whose cobblestone alleys are lined with quaint timber-framed buildings ornamented with colourful flower boxes. As you walk, the aroma of freshly made Black Forest cake fills the air, beckoning you to indulge in this delectable local delicacy.

Next, go further into the forest, where old trees tell stories from decades past. Follow meandering trails that lead to secret glens and isolated waterfalls, each providing a moment of peace in the forest. Keep your eyes out for animals dashing through the underbrush, including secretive deer and playful foxes.

Visit a typical Black Forest homestead or museum to learn about generations-old customs and crafts. Admire finely carved cuckoo clocks, a hallmark of the region's famed workmanship, and perhaps try your hand at creating your own wooden masterpiece.

As the day comes to an end, have a delicious lunch at a local tavern, where you can eat savoury foods like robust stews and smoked sausages while sipping on a cool glass of local beer or wine. Then, as evening falls over the forest, bid farewell to this lovely domain and return to Basel.

Colmar (France)

Begin your travel in the early morning from Basel, which is only a short distance from Colmar. As you cross the border into France, the beautiful route reveals the breathtaking scenery of the Alsace wine region, with rolling vineyards colouring the countryside in shades of green and gold. The ride itself becomes a visual feast, setting the stage for the splendour that awaits in Colmar.

Upon arriving, become lost in the maze of cobblestone streets that meander through the town's ancient centre. Each turn offers a new gem, from half-timbered cottages with colourful shutters to small eateries hidden behind archways. Take a leisurely stroll around the canal-lined neighbourhoods, where flowering flowers pour from window boxes, giving a splash of colour to the already beautiful scenery.

One of the attractions of every visit to Colmar is the renowned Unterlinden Museum, which has an extraordinary collection of artwork spanning decades. Admire treasures by painters like as Grünewald and Picasso, and don't miss out on seeing the Isenheim Altarpiece, a hauntingly beautiful work that captivates visitors with its meticulous detail and evocative strength.

After immersing yourself in art and history, enjoy Alsace's gastronomic pleasures. Visit a local bakery to try flaky tarte flambée or have choucroute garnie, a typical dish of sauerkraut, sausages, and potatoes. Wash it all down with a glass of fresh Alsatian wine, made from the vineyards that cover the surrounding slopes.

As the day comes to a close, take a minute to enjoy Colmar's ageless appeal. Wander around the crowded markets, where sellers offer fresh food and artisan items, or simply find a quiet area along the canal to watch the world go by. And when the sun sets over the roofs, creating a golden light over the town, you'll see why Colmar is regarded as one of France's most beautiful cities.

Lucerne

As you leave Basel, the ride gets more scenic, with rolling hills and little towns dotting the countryside.

When you arrive in Lucerne, you will be welcomed by the stunning sight of Lake Lucerne, with its clean waters reflecting the gorgeous mountains that surround it. The historic Kapellbrücke, or Chapel Bridge, sweeps beautifully across the lake, decked with vibrant flowers and rich in history. Walking along this centuries-old wooden bridge seems like travelling back in time, as you admire the exquisite paintings and absorb up the tranquil ambiance.

Exploring Lucerne's Old Town is like travelling through a living museum, with well-preserved mediaeval buildings and cobblestone pathways guiding you through the city's rich history. The towering spires of the Hofkirche, or Church of St. Leodegar, draw attention, but hidden jewels like the Museggmauer provide panoramic views of the city underneath.

No trip to Lucerne is complete without a cruise on Lake Lucerne itself. Board a classic paddle boat and float across the crystal-clear river, surrounded by the breathtaking Swiss Alps. The air is fresh, the view is stunning, and each moment is like a postcard come to life.

The Swiss Museum of Transport is a must-see for anybody looking to experience Swiss culture. Here, you may explore the intriguing world of transport, from historic trains to interactive exhibitions exhibiting the country's inventive spirit.

As the day comes to an end, you may find yourself lingering on the banks of Lake Lucerne, watching the sun fall below the horizon in a blaze of colour.

Swiss Countryside

As you leave the city, you can feel the excitement growing as the rich beauty of the Swiss countryside opens before you. Every turn will reveal picture-perfect views of rolling hills, picturesque villages, and calm lakes.

Visit the lovely town of Lauterbrunnen, which is located in a valley surrounded by towering cliffs and flowing waterfalls. You may enjoy the cool mountain air while enjoying leisurely walks along the well-marked hiking routes, which provide stunning views of the renowned Swiss Alps.

Continue your journey to the lovely town of Grindelwald, which is famed for its breathtaking alpine scenery and outdoor activities. Whether you prefer to take a picturesque cable car journey to the peak of Mount First or simply relax and absorb in the quiet atmosphere, Grindelwald offers an outstanding experience for both nature lovers and adventure seekers.

No trip to the Swiss countryside is complete without partaking in the region's gastronomic offerings. Treat yourself to a delicious Swiss fondue or classic raclette at a cosy mountain hut, where you can savour the flavours of local cheeses and freshly baked bread while taking in the spectacular backdrop.

As the sun sets, wave farewell to the Swiss countryside and return to Basel, full of memories of a day spent experiencing the region's natural beauty and cultural riches.

CHAPTER 9: PRACTICAL INFORMATION

Weather And Best Time To Visit

Spring (March-May) in Basel provides moderate weather and beautiful flowers. The city comes alive with outdoor events, festivals, and cultural activities. The weather is mostly good, with temperatures ranging from 10°C to 20°C. This is a good time to visit Basel's parks, take a stroll along the Rhine River, and enjoy outdoor cafés.

Summer (June-August) is the most popular tourism season in Basel. The weather is pleasant and sunny, with temperatures ranging from 20°C to 30°C (68°F to 86°F). This is the ideal season to enjoy outdoor activities like swimming in the Rhine, attending open-air concerts and festivals, and visiting the city's numerous museums and galleries.

Autumn (September–November) brings milder weather and colourful foliage to Basel. The temperature remains pleasant, ranging from 10°C to 20°C (50°F to 68°F). This is an excellent time to come if you prefer less crowds and want to enjoy the city's cultural offers without the summer throng.

Winter in Basel (December-February) is frigid but lovely, especially during the holiday season. Temperatures normally range between -2°C and 6°C (28°F to 43°F). The city is decked up in holiday lights and decorations, and you can go ice skating, visit traditional Christmas markets, and warm up in cafes with hot chocolate.

The ideal time to visit Basel is based on your choices. If you prefer warm weather and outdoor activities, summer is the best season to visit. If you prefer milder temps and less tourists, consider visiting in the spring or autumn. Winter is ideal for enjoying Basel's festive atmosphere and winter activities.

Currency and Payment

Switzerland's national currency is the Swiss Franc (CHF), which is divisible into 100 centimes (commonly known as "rappen"). Prices will be presented as "CHF" or simply "Fr."

Both cash and cards are generally accepted in Basel, yet each has its benefits:

Cash:

- Good for smaller purchases: While most stores and restaurants take credit cards, certain smaller businesses, such as street sellers or bakeries, may prefer cash.
- Taxis and public transportation: Although some public transportation alternatives take credit cards, having cash on hand is always useful for taxis or unforeseen circumstances.
- Tipping: Tipping in Switzerland is typically 5-10%, and it is frequently done in cash.

Cards:

- Convenience and security: Carrying fewer francs reduces the risk of losing them. Major credit cards such as Visa, MasterCard, and Maestro are frequently accepted.
- Improved exchange rates: Paying in CHF with your card typically results in a better conversion rate than converting currency beforehand.

Tips for Using Cards:

- Inform your bank. To avoid any potential complications, notify your bank ahead of time that you will be using your card in Switzerland.

- Choose the correct card: Look for a card that has no international transaction fees or offers competitive exchange rates.

- Dynamic Currency Conversion (DCC) When making a purchase, be careful of DCC, which may provide an unfavourable exchange rate. Always opt to be charged in the local currency (CHF).

Exchanging Currencies:

- ATMs: The most convenient method to receive CHF is to withdraw it from a Basel ATM. Look for ATMs that are part of your bank's network to avoid unnecessary costs.

- Currency exchange offices: While not the most cost-effective solution, exchange offices can provide some initial cash upon arrival.

Language

In Basel, you may hear the melodic cadence of Swiss German, the official language used by the residents. Its peculiar vernacular provides a delightful touch to ordinary discussions while emphasising the city's particular personality. However, be prepared to face a potpourri of other languages, including French, English, and Italian. Basel, with its closeness to the linguistic richness of France, Germany, and Switzerland, is a melting pot where diverse tongues coexist together.

As you immerse yourself in the lively cultural environment, you'll learn that language is more than simply a mode of communication; it's a reflection of history, culture, and identity. Whether you're negotiating in the busy marketplaces of Marktplatz or savouring a tasty Swiss cuisine at a cosy café, language serves as a channel for shared experiences and important connections.5

Greetings & Farewells:

Grüezi: This friendly "hello" is your go-to greeting, anytime of day. It literally means "may God greet you."

Guete Morge/Tag/Abig: More formal greetings for good morning, day, and evening respectively.

Uf Widerluege: This literally translates to "on see-again" and is a warm goodbye.

Tschüss/Ciao/Salü: Informal goodbyes, similar to "bye" in various languages.

Essential Interactions:

Entschuldigung: Excuse me, essential for navigating crowds and politely getting someone's attention.

Bitte: Please, always use this when making requests.

Danke/Merci: Thank you, with "merci" being the more widely used Swiss expression.

Merci vilmal: Thanks a lot! This literally means "thanks many times" and shows extra appreciation.

Spreche Sie Englisch?: Do you speak English? Useful if you get stuck, but locals appreciate the effort to speak Swiss German.

Navigating & Asking for Help:

Wo ist...? Where is...? Fill in the blank with your destination (toilet, museum, etc.).

Kannst du mir helfen?: Can you help me?

Wie komme ich nach...? How do I get to...?

Entschuldigung, können Sie das bitte langsamer sagen?: Excuse me, could you please say that slower?

Dining & Shopping:

En guete: Enjoy your meal! A polite wish before digging in.

Was kostet das?: How much does this cost?

Kann ich bitte die Rechnung?: Can I please have the bill?

Kann ich zahlen?: Can I pay?

Beyond the Basics:

Proscht/Pröschtli: Cheers! Raise your glass and enjoy your drink with this toast.

Äbä, genau: Yeah, right, exactly. A casual agreement or confirmation.

Alles klar?: Is everything alright? A friendly check-in.

Gern gschee!: You're welcome! Literally means "gladly done."

Tip: Don't worry about perfect pronunciation! Locals appreciate the effort and will happily correct you if needed. Most importantly, smile, be friendly, and have fun using your newfound Swiss German skills!

Safety Tips

1. **Stay mindful of Your Surroundings:** Whether you're touring the city centre or meandering through calmer neighbourhoods, you should always be mindful of your surroundings.

2. **Secure Your stuff:** Keep your stuff safe to avoid theft. Keep your belongings safe by carrying a cross-body bag or a money belt, especially in crowded settings or on public transit.

3. **Use Reliable Transportation:** Stick to reputable modes of transportation, such as licenced taxis or public transit. Avoid using unmarked taxis or accepting rides from strangers.

4. **Stay in Well-lighted locations at Night**: If you're out after dark, stay on well-lighted streets and avoid dimly lit or empty locations.

5. **Be Wary of exchanging Sensitive Personal Information:** Avoid exchanging sensitive personal information with strangers, particularly financial or housing information. When using an ATM, exercise caution and keep your PIN hidden.

6. **Follow Local Laws and Customs:** Familiarise yourself with Basel's local laws and customs to ensure you follow the law and respect local traditions.

7. **Emergency Preparedness**: Know Basel's emergency contact numbers, which include the local police, ambulance, and fire departments. Maintain a list of critical contacts in case of an emergency.

8. **Stay Hydrated and Sun Protected:** Wear sunscreen, a hat, and sunglasses throughout the warmer months to stay hydrated and protected from the sun.

9. **Consider obtaining travel insurance** that covers medical emergencies, trip cancellations, and theft to give you peace of mind throughout your vacation.

10. **Trust Your Instincts**: If anything does not seem right, follow your instincts and leave the situation. If you feel insecure, do not hesitate to seek aid from authorities or locals.

Local Etiquette

1. Punctuality is highly valued in Switzerland, so come on time for appointments, meetings, and social functions. Being late without a legitimate excuse might be perceived as rude.

2. When meeting someone, a hard handshake is the customary greeting. Use titles and last names unless specifically requested to use first names.

3. While many people in Basel understand English, it is courteous to acquire a few simple words in Swiss German or French, the two most often spoken languages in the area.

4. Swiss culture emphasises personal space, therefore avoid standing too near to others or engaging in excessively familiar behaviour, especially with new acquaintances.

5. Basel is noted for its refined elegance, so dress neatly and conservatively, especially if you're attending a cultural event or a business conference.

6. When dining out, wait to be seated and keep your hands on the table, rather than in your lap. Say "Prost" (cheers) before taking your first drink, and eat with utensils rather than your hands.

7. Tipping is less usual and anticipated in Switzerland than in other nations. A service fee is frequently included on the bill, although it is still customary to round up the amount or offer a modest tip for exemplary service.

8. Switzerland is famed for its stunning natural environments, therefore avoid littering and observe recycling standards. Smoking is also prohibited in many public locations, therefore follow designated smoking zones.

9. Show respect for Swiss cultures and traditions, particularly religious practices. Avoid discussing contentious issues like politics or religion until you know the individual and the context of the conversation.

Packing Essentials

1. Comfortable walking shoes are recommended since Basel's picturesque streets, bridges, and riverbanks are best explored on foot. Pack a pair of durable, comfy shoes to keep your feet happy while you walk around.

2. Because Switzerland's weather may be unpredictable, it's best to carry layers. Pack a combination of lightweight clothing for warmer days and sweaters or jackets for chilly evenings or unexpected rain showers.

3. Don't forget to bring adapters and chargers to keep your electronic gadgets connected and charged up during your journey.

4. Stay hydrated when exploring Basel by bringing a reusable water bottle. There are lots of drinking fountains throughout the city where you may refill it for free.

5. Keep your passport, tickets, hotel bookings, and any essential visas organised and readily available. It's also a good idea to keep some Swiss Francs on hand for little purchases and public transit.

6. A compact daypack or tote bag might be useful for carrying basics such as water, food, a camera, and any mementos you find along the road.

7. If you're visiting Basel during the summer, remember to bring sunscreen and sunglasses to protect yourself from UV rays while you're touring.

8. While it's exciting to explore new areas on your own, having a guidebook or map of Basel may help you navigate your way about and learn about the city's history and attractions.

9. Bring any required drugs in their original containers, as well as a basic first aid kit for minor emergencies or illnesses.

10. Finally, make sure you have travel insurance for your trip and have a list of emergency contact information, such as local authorities and your embassy or consulate.

CHAPTER 10: USEFUL RESOURCES

Tourist Information Centers

Tourist Information Barfüsserplatz: This is Basel's primary tourist information centre, located in the heart of the old town on Barfüsser Platz. It is open every day from 9:00 a.m. to 6:30 p.m. (with reduced hours on Sundays). The personnel here can assist you with anything from scheduling excursions and accommodations to locating the best restaurants and shops. *Tel: +41 61 268 68 68. www.basel.com/en/attractions/tourist-information-office-in-the-stadtcasino-at-barfuesserplatz-308ae64ba5*

The Basel Tourism Management Office is located in Aeschenvorstadt 36, a little further from the city centre. However, it still provides a richness of information and services and is open Monday through Friday from 8:30 a.m. to 5:30 p.m. *www.tourisme-mulhouse.com Tel: +41 61 268 68 68*

The Tourist Information Kiosk at the SBB railway station: This kiosk is an excellent choice if you arrive in Basel by rail. It is available everyday from 8:00 a.m. to 8:00 p.m. and can offer you with general information about the city as well as assistance in purchasing public transit tickets.

Navigation Apps

Maps.me: This free tool allows you to download detailed maps of Basel for offline use, saving you money on roaming charges and guaranteeing you can navigate even when you don't have access to the internet. It also contains places of interest (POIs) such as restaurants, ATMs, and public transit stations.

SwitzerlandMobility: The Swiss tourist board's app focuses on outdoor activities, including comprehensive hiking and bicycle paths in the Basel region. It also offers an offline map option.

Fahrplan+: Fahrplan+ is the official app for the Swiss public transport system, providing real-time information on bus, tram and train timetables, delays and routes in Basel and beyond. It also allows you to buy tickets using the app.

Moovit is a worldwide app that allows you to plan trips using many modes of transportation, including public transportation, walking, and cycling. It also offers real arrival times and instructions.

Emergency Contacts

These connections may include local authorities, medical services, and trustworthy persons who can assist in various crises.

First and foremost, become familiar with the local emergency number, which in Switzerland is 112. This number will link you to emergency services such as police, fire, and medical aid. Memorise it or save it on your phone for easy access.

Also, make sure you know how to reach your country's embassy or consulate in Basel. They can assist you in the event of a passport loss, legal difficulties, or other nationality-related crises.

If you are staying at a hotel or Airbnb, keep the contact information for the property management or front desk handy. They can help you with local emergency procedures, medical services, or any other pressing issues that may occur during your stay.

It's also a good idea to have the contact information for a local doctor or medical facility in case of an emergency or unexpected illness. This guarantees that you may promptly seek medical treatment if necessary.

Finally, advise a trustworthy friend or family member of your vacation arrangements, including your itinerary and emergency contact information. This allows them to provide remote support and assistance in the event of an unforeseen incident.

CONCLUSION

Top 10 Things To Do

1. **Explore the Old Town**: Walk through Basel's cobblestone streets, where mediaeval architecture meets vibrant modern life. Admire the stately Basel Minster, wander along the Rhine River, and find hidden treasures in the small lanes.

2. **Visit the Art institutions**: Immerse yourself in Basel's vibrant art scene by visiting internationally recognised institutions such as the Fondation Beyeler and Kunstmuseum Basel. Admire works by Picasso, Monet, and Van Gogh while discovering the city's cultural legacy.

3. **Rhine River boat**: Take a picturesque boat down the Rhine River, which offers stunning views of the city skyline and neighbouring surroundings. Relax on deck as you pass by historic sites and charming communities.

4. **Marktplatz Market**: Indulge your senses at the busy Marktplatz market, where residents come to buy fresh

vegetables, handmade crafts, and traditional Swiss cuisine. Try local specialties such as cheese fondue, chocolate truffles, and freshly baked bread.

5. **Basel Zoo** is home to around 6,000 animals from throughout the world. Get up close and personal with lions, giraffes, and penguins while learning about conservation initiatives via interactive exhibits.

6. **Rheinfelden Thermal Baths**: Enjoy a day of leisure at the Rheinfelden Thermal Baths, located just a short drive from Basel. Soak in restorative hot springs, relax with a massage, and take in the breathtaking views of the Rhine Valley.

7. **Day Trip to Rhine** Take a day trip to Rhine Falls, Europe's biggest waterfall, located near Basel. Admire the thunderous waterfall, take a boat trip to the falls' base, and explore picturesque paths for breathtaking vistas.

8. **Tinguely Fountain**: Admire the quirky Tinguely Fountain, a dynamic artwork located in Theaterplatz. Swiss artist Jean Tinguely designed the fountain, which contains fun water jets and moving metal sculptures that entertain visitors of all ages.

9. **Fasnacht Carnival**: Take in the vivid energy of Basel's Fasnacht Carnival, one of Switzerland's largest and oldest. Join the fun as colourful parades, spectacular costumes and vibrant music fill the streets during this yearly event.

10. **Climb to the top of the Basel Munster Tower** to enjoy panoramic views of the city and surrounding countryside. Take in the stunning views of the Rhine River, Black Forest, and Swiss Alps from this landmark location.

3 Days Itinerary

Day 1: Exploring Basel's Historic Heart.
Begin your day with a visit to the Basel Minster, a breathtaking Gothic church that dominates the cityscape. Admire the beautiful construction and ascend the tower for panoramic views of Basel and the Rhine River.

After that, meander around the Old Town's lovely streets, which are lined with attractive squares, mediaeval houses, and cosy cafes. Don't miss a trip down the Rhine promenade, which is adorned with colourful buildings and bustling marketplaces.

For lunch, try some classic Swiss food at a nearby eatery. Try fondue or raclette for a taste of traditional Swiss flavours.

In the afternoon, head to the Kunstmuseum Basel, one of Switzerland's most renowned art museums. As you tour the museum's huge collection, you'll see masterpieces by Picasso, Monet, and van Gogh, among others.

End your day with a relaxed meal at a riverbank restaurant, where you can eat exquisite Swiss cuisine while overlooking the Rhine.

Day Two: Cultural exploration and relaxation.
Begin your day by visiting the Fondation Beyeler, which is located in Riehen, just outside Basel. This world-class art museum is located in a gorgeous park and houses works by contemporary masters like Picasso, Rothko, and Warhol.

After that, return to Basel and spend some time discovering the city's lively cultural scene. Visit the Museum Tinguely to view the whimsical and dynamic sculptures of Swiss artist Jean Tinguely.

For lunch, visit Markthalle Basel, a lively market hall with food vendors serving a wide range of different cuisines.

In the afternoon, take a leisurely boat tour down the Rhine River. Sit back and take in the scenery as you glide by historic sites and lovely landscapes.

In the evening, relax in one of Basel's famed thermal baths, such as the old Roman-Irish Bath or Aquabasilea, a contemporary spa complex. Relax in the relaxing waves and revitalise your body and mind.

Day 3: Day trip to the Swiss countryside.
Today, leave the city for a day excursion to experience the beautiful Swiss countryside.

Begin your day with a lovely train ride to the picturesque hamlet of Lauterbrunnen in the Bernese Oberland area. Lauterbrunnen is a nature lover's dream, with breathtaking waterfalls and spectacular mountain landscapes.

From Lauterbrunnen, take the cogwheel train to Wengen, a lovely alpine hamlet. Enjoy amazing views of the surrounding peaks while indulging in some classic Swiss food at a nearby restaurant.

After lunch, make your way to the landmark Jungfraujoch, commonly known as the "Top of Europe." Take the cogwheel train to Europe's highest railway station and enjoy breathtaking views of the Swiss Alps.

In the afternoon, visit Jungfraujoch's attractions, which include the Ice Palace and the Sphinx Observatory. Experience the breathtaking grandeur of the glacial scenery before returning to Basel in the evening.

7 Days Itinerary

Day One: Arrival and Exploration

Basel captivates visitors with its combination of old-world elegance and modern energy. Take a leisurely stroll along the banks of the Rhine River, where colourful buildings reflect in the water and bustling cafés invite you to have a cup of Swiss coffee. Explore the Altstadt (Old Town), which features cobblestone streets and mediaeval architecture, stopping to view monuments such as the Basel Minster and Rathaus. In the evening, enjoy a fantastic supper with Swiss favourites such as fondue or raclette.

Day Two: Art and Culture.

Basel is known for its vibrant art scene, so today is spent touring its world-class museums and galleries. Begin with the Kunstmuseum Basel, which has an amazing collection of European art spanning centuries. Continue to the Fondation Beyeler, which is situated in a spectacular Renzo Piano-designed structure and features works by contemporary masters such as Picasso, Monet, and Rothko. In the evening, see a show at the Theatre Basel or attend a classical music at the famed Musiksaal.

Day Three: Rhine River Cruise and Botanical Gardens.

Take a picturesque cruise down the Rhine River, enjoying panoramic views of Basel and the surrounding countryside. Along the journey, you'll see quaint villages, beautiful vineyards, and picturesque castles perched on slopes. Afterward, visit the Basel Botanical Garden, a calm paradise with hundreds of plant varieties from all over the world. Take a leisurely stroll through themed gardens such as alpine, tropical, and medicinal, and eat a picnic in the natural setting.

Day 4: Trip to Lucerne.

Take advantage of Basel's handy position and plan a day excursion to Lucerne, which is only a short train journey away. Admire the renowned Chapel Bridge that spans the Reuss River, stop at the Lion Monument to honour Swiss guards who died during the French Revolution, and stroll through the mediaeval Old Town's lovely squares and lanes. Don't pass up the opportunity to take a magnificent boat tour on Lake Lucerne, surrounded by breathtaking alpine views.

Day 5: Culinary delights and Market Exploration

Begin your day by visiting Basel's lively Marktplatz, where local farmers and craftsmen sell fresh vegetables, cheese, baked goods, and crafts. Enjoy a classic Swiss breakfast of crusty bread, cheese, and cured meats before perusing the market booths. In the afternoon, take a gourmet walking tour to sample wonderful Swiss chocolates, pastries, and other delights while learning about Basel's gastronomic traditions.

Day 6: Basel Zoo & Shopping

Spend the morning at the Basel Zoo, one of Switzerland's oldest and largest, which houses a wide collection of animals from all over the world. Explore beautifully planted habitats, see rare creatures up close, and attend informative presentations and feeding sessions. Spend the afternoon shopping on Freie Strasse, Basel's principal shopping strip, which is dotted with luxury boutiques, department stores and specialist shops selling everything from Swiss watches to designer couture.

Day 7: Outdoor Adventures & Farewell

On your final day in Basel, get outside to see the city's stunning parks and leisure places. Rent a bike and ride along the Rhine River's bicycle pathways, pausing to enjoy panoramic vistas and quaint riverfront cafes. Alternatively, go hiking in the adjacent Black Forest or Jura Mountains, where you can immerse yourself in nature and breathe pure mountain air. In the evening, say goodbye to Basel with a magnificent meal overlooking the Rhine, toasting to a fantastic week of travel and discovery in this enchanting Swiss city.

Maps

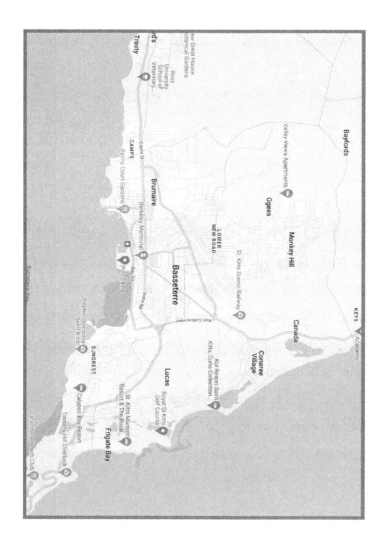

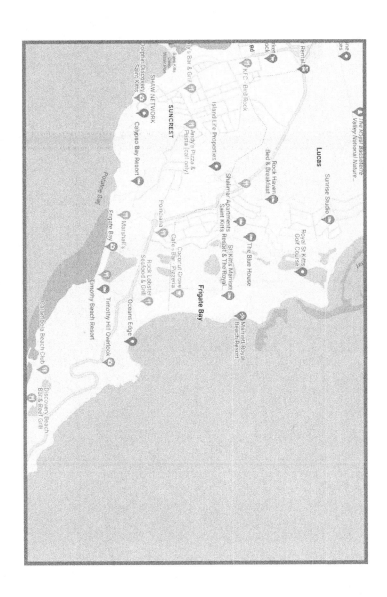

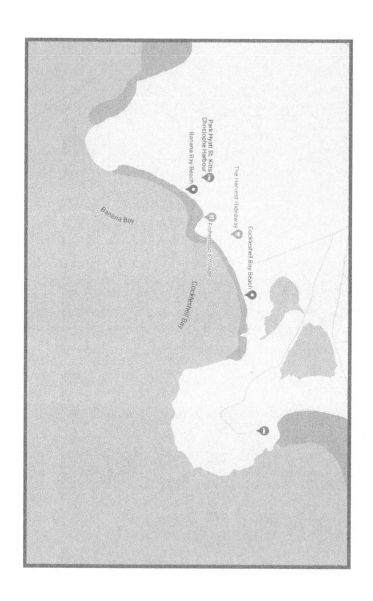

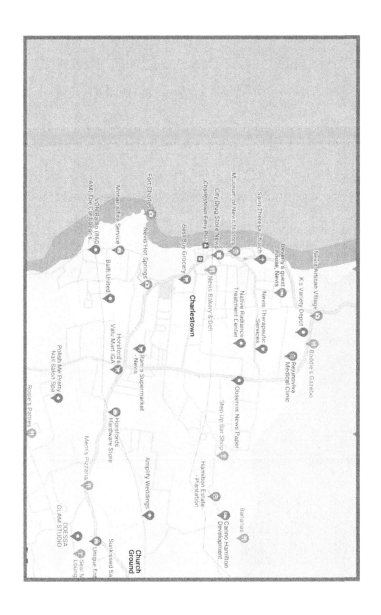

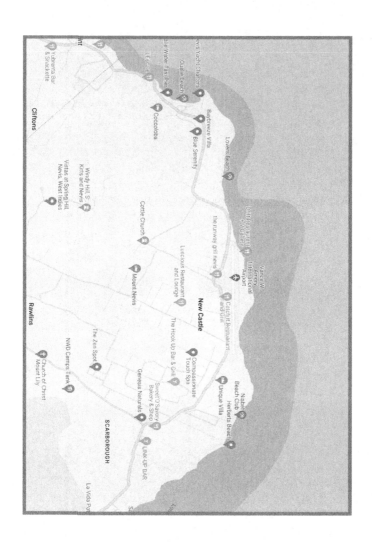

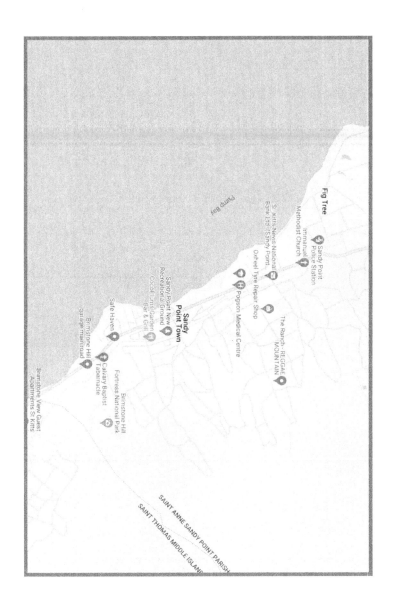

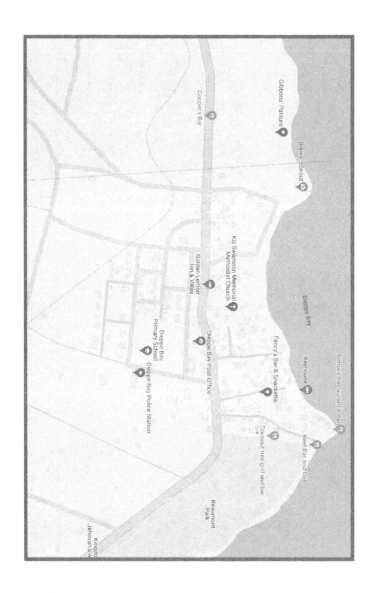

Printed in Great Britain
by Amazon

42535473R00076